It's Just My Personality

Exploring and Explaining
Myers-Briggs Personality Types

by Rachel Grant
M.A. Counseling Psychology

It's Just My Personality: Exploring and Explaining Myers-Briggs Personality Types

Copyright © 2012 by Rachel Grant

All rights reserved. No part of this book may be used or reproduced by any means, graphic, electronic, or mechanical, including photocopying, recording, taping or by any information storage retrieval system without the written permission of the publisher except in the case of brief quotations embodied in critical articles and reviews.

Because of the dynamic nature of the Internet, any web addresses or links contained in this book may have changed since publication and may no longer be valid. The views expressed in this work are solely those of the author and do not necessarily reflect the views of the publisher, and the publisher hereby disclaims any responsibility for them.

ISBN-13: 978-1481256865
ISBN-10: 1481256866

Printed in the United States.

Contents

Part 1: Exploring Myers-Briggs 4
Part 2: Being an Extrovert 6
Part 3: Being an Introvert 8
Part 4: Being a Sensing Type 11
Part 5: Being an Intuition Type 13
Part 6: Being a Thinking Type 16
Part 7: Being a Feeling Type 18
Part 8: Being a Judging Type 21
Part 9: Being a Perceiving Type 24
Part 10: Conclusion 27

Part 1: Exploring Myers-Briggs

I've long been fascinated by the Myers-Briggs Personality Test, and I often start off having new clients take this test to get a general sense of how they tick.

This questionnaire, originally developed by Katharine Cook Briggs and Isabel Briggs Myers, was designed to measure the psychological preferences in **how people perceive the world and make decisions** as informed by the theories proposed by Carl Jung in his book, <u>Psychological Types</u>.

The four dichotomies that make up the personalities types are:

Extraversion (E) - Introversion (I)

Sensing (S) - Intuition (N)

Thinking (T) - Feeling (F)

Judging (J) - Perceiving (P)

These can then be combined to result in a four letter personality type (e.g., INFJ, ESTP).

While this particular personality test doesn't cover all of the bases, it certainly highlights key characteristics and tendencies of behavior and perception that are commonly shared among those with a particular personality type. Understanding how some of our behavior, attitudes, and perspectives are driven by personality can be very useful and liberating.

I will be breaking down each type to explore the way a person of that personality type might perceive the world and make decisions.

I encourage you to take the Jung Typology test at www.humanmetrics.com, so you can know which types to pay particular attention to, but I encourage you to read all of the following sections as well. Knowing how the other half sees the world can also be very useful!

TIP: When taking the test, don't over-think your answers—just go with your first, gut response!

Part 2: Being an Extrovert

It's 7:00 AM. Your boss calls you at home and tells you to take the day off—everything is covered. What will you do with your unanticipated free day?

If you said, "Go out with some friends, catch dinner with some folks, plan a group outing," you are likely an Extrovert.

Being an Extrovert is not so much about whether or not you are outgoing or comfortable in groups. It is more about **where you get your energy from.**

As an Extrovert, you are energized:

- By the external world of people, activities, and things
- When trying things out
- By interaction with others
- By talking things out

This means that you are recharged and invigorated by social interaction and prefer talking through ideas rather than going off on your own to reflect.

One trap here though is to end up thinking that every idea shared needs to be acted on. I call it "Extrovert overload." As you begin "talking things out," you hit upon idea after idea—"We could do it this way...", "Or how about this...!"

Before you know it, you have twenty ideas on the table and are feeling overwhelmed—either not knowing which one to choose or thinking you have to do it all. To avoid this, think of your "talking things out" time as a bit of a download rather than as an action list.

At work and play, the Extrovert:

- Seeks variety and action, can get bored easily
- Wants to be with others
- Prefers interests that have breadth
- Are after-thinkers

For the Extrovert, alone time is still important, but it drains energy rather than restores. If you find yourself feeling run down, tired, or bored, recharge by getting into action or going out and being around others.

Finally, when it comes to communication, Extroverts:

- Require less personal space
- Speak louder and more quickly than Introverts
- Use more physical gestures and facial animation than Introverts
- Like to meet face-to-face
- Blurts!

Understanding your communication style is extremely helpful—especially when you are communicating with an Introvert, who will prefer to listen to a few ideas, go off and reflect and then return to develop a plan of action.

Extroverts can come across as overbearing, intimidating, or overwhelming. So, learning when to turn it down a notch, to tune into the energy level of the person you are communicating with, and developing some skills to avoid blurting out whatever is one your mind are all good places to start for Extroverts.

Part 3: Being an Introvert

It's 7:00 AM. Your boss calls you at home and tells you to take the day off—everything is covered. What will you do with your unanticipated free day?

If you said, "Chill out at home alone, read a book, go for a solitary stroll," you are likely an Introvert.

Being an Introvert is not so much about being shy or not outgoing. It is more about **where you get your energy from.**

As an Introvert, you are energized:

- By the internal world of reflection and contemplation
- When taking in information or ideas
- By quiet time alone
- By thinking things through

This means that you are recharged and invigorated by time alone and prefer to have time to reflect and think things over before acting. Therefore, it is extremely important to carve out time for yourself during the week to get away. Introverts who do not make time for reflection and solitude usually pay the price—they crash (either physically or mentally). Being with others drains an Introvert's energy level, so it is very important to set aside time to recharge!

At work and play, the Introvert:

- Seeks quiet time for concentration; needs time alone
- Prefers interests that have depth
- Are fore-thinkers
- Sometimes hesitates to act

One trap that Introverts fall into (aside from overscheduling) is that they spend too much time in reflection, become paralyzed, and find it difficult to get into action. They begin to think "too much" and get stuck. To avoid this trap, it can be helpful to set out a time limit for your reflection period (e.g. "I'll make a decision on this by Friday").

Finally, when it comes to communication, Introverts:

- Pause before responding
- Process information internally
- Prefer written over verbal communication
- Prefer to work independently

Understanding your communication style is extremely helpful—especially when you are communicating with an Extrovert, who will prefer to talk things out, which can leave an Introvert feeling drained and overwhelmed.

Introverts can come across as distant or unengaged. So, developing the skill of being clear that you have heard the communication and then asking for time to reflect can be a real life saver for Introverts. Avoid the pitfall of trying to respond too quickly. You will usually regret your answer and have to do more work in the long run.

If you are an I interacting with an E:

- Allow E's to process with you
- Understand that everything said isn't acted upon
- Offer outlets for stimulation and connection

If you are an E interacting with an I:

- Allow I's time to think alone
- Don't assume I's aren't thinking just because they aren't talking
- Offer outlets for solitude and rejuvenation

When it comes to E's and I's getting along, these two graphics sum it up nicely!

Part 4: Being a Sensing Type

How would you define "time"?

If you said, "It's a system of measurement or a limited period or interval," you are likely a Sensing type ("Sensor").

Whereas the first dichotomy—E's and I's—was all about how we are energized, this next type is all about **what we pay attention to.**

As a Sensor, you pay attention to:

- Practical facts
- Details
- Realities
- Past and present
- Specifics
- What is actual

This means that in any given situation, you tend to first evaluate the facts, want to gather the details or specifics of the situation, and want to make decisions based on these facts and on reality. Sensors prefer to pay attention to what is right in front of them, relying more heavily on the present facts/reality and past experiences (learning) to make decisions.

At work and play, the Sensor:

- Prefers using learned skills and an established ways of doing things
- Pays attention to details
- Makes few factual errors
- Focuses on what works now
- Distrusts inspiration

Sensors are the people we go to when we need clear and concise information. They take pleasure in the details, can see things that others miss, and can develop solid systems and processes to get the job done.

One trap here, though, is that Sensors can become rigid and stuck in his/her ways once s/he has found (or has been trained in) a way of doing things. This can lead to stagnation and, worse, discomfort with or resistance to change. So, it will be important to cultivate some skills around flexibility and openness to change so that both your work and play life do not become stagnant.

Finally, when it comes to perception and orientation, Sensors:

- Rely on their five senses (on experience and actual data)
- Focus on present enjoyment
- Are oriented toward living life as it is

Sensors are connected to what is currently happening and are oriented towards the past and present, which can be a real strength. They pay close attention to physical reality—what they can see, hear, taste, smell, and touch. As a result, they learn best by first connecting to the practical use (how the knowledge will be applied) and then by experience (doing) rather than being shown or told.

Sensors can sometimes come across as overly practical or realistic to the point of unimaginative. So, it will be important to develop the skill of embracing and encouraging the creativity and idealism of others around you, even if it may not seem to be of the highest importance to you.

Part 5: Being an Intuition Type

How would you define "time"?

If you said, "A way of measuring your journey, keeping track of your experiences, or provides an opportunity to explore" you are likely an Intuition type ("Intuitive").

Again, as with the Sensors, this type is all about **what we pay attention to.**

As an Intuitive, you pay attention to:

- Insights
- Patterns of ideas
- Possibilities
- What could be
- The big picture

This means that you prefer thinking about the overall scheme of things, looking for inter-related connections, exploring possibilities and opportunities. You are less inclined to notice the exact details or facts of a situation. Instead, thinking about what could be, what might happen, or what is possible is more appealing.

At work and play, the Intuitive:

- Prefers adding new skills, dislikes doing the same thing
- Considers how things could be improved
- Looks at the "big picture"
- Follows inspiration
- Works in bursts of energy

The Intuitive likes following the rabbit trail to some extent. Once latched upon an idea, the Intuitive is happy to follow the threads to see where the ideas, information may lead. They my catch ahold of an idea and be unable to let it go until following it through to what seems like a natural end. They are innovative and can see all of the pieces of a puzzle.

Another key element of being an Intuitive is that you work in bursts of energy. I like to think of this as the **"Intuitive's Energy Cycle."** You will enter into a stage of high productivity, getting many tasks done, be filled with high energy, and be fully engaged. Then you will, sometimes quite literally, crash. Your motivation will wane, interest will decline, and energy dissipates making the couch your favorite spot to be.

One trap here is to interpret these drops as representing dysfunction, as a threat to your success or overall outcomes, or, in simpler terms, that you are a loser who is never going to get anywhere. Our world is not really built for the energy cycle of Intuitives. The more accepted behavior is to go, go, go – do, do, do.

Still, don't fret! Instead, it is important to come to an understanding of this cycle and embrace it rather than fight against it and to also learn to communicate with those you work and play with about these down times as being your way to rejuvenate and refill your tank so that further insights and inspiration can come again— and they will come again! You will recharge and get back to work.

Finally, when it comes to perception and orientation, Intuitives:

- Rely on their "sixth sense" (possibilities and inspiration)
- Focus on future achievement
- Are oriented toward changing and rearranging life

Intuitives love to shake things up. Patterns and routines are a major buzz kill. Instead, they love to explore new and unusual ideas. They are also motivated more so by future outcomes than immediate present rewards.

Intuitives can come across as ungrounded, disorganized, or not connected to reality. They can sometimes seem indecisive as well. So, it is important to develop the skill of following your intuition, creating space to chase an inspired thought, while being able to bring things back to the present so that your strengths of insight and perception can shine through.

If you are an S interacting with an N:

- Use the N's ability to sense possibilities and opportunities to broaden the playing field
- Allow N's to explore ideas, follow their intuition—resist your temptation to distrust inspiration

If you are an N interacting with an S:

- Provide details and information before asking for a decision
- Offer S's some here and now benefits, facts, details—bring things back to the present

Part 6: Being a Thinking Type

Think about a boss, professor or supervisor you enjoyed working with. What was it about them that made them effective?

If you said, "She was really good at communicating information clearly, set specific goals and objectives. There were some things I didn't like, but overall, she was very effective and treated me fairly," you are likely a Thinking type ("Thinker").

This next type is all about **what we base our decisions on.**

As a Thinker, you base your decisions on:

- Non-personal logic
- Objective information
- An outcome that "makes sense"
- Logical implications

This means that you lean towards basing decisions on measurable criteria. Decisions usually get made after evaluating the pros and cons of a given situation. For the most part, you strive to make decisions objectively using non-personal logic. This isn't to say that emotion or feelings never enter into the equation for Thinkers; it just means that logic and objective information are more heavily relied upon.

At work and play, the Thinker:

- Behaves in a brief and businesslike manner
- Acts impersonally; tends to be firm
- Treats others fairly and needs to be treated fairly
- May hurt other people's feelings without knowing it
- Tends to be firm

The Thinker tends to enjoy technical or scientific fields and thrives in environments where the culture is direct and structured. "Fairness" is an extremely important concept for Thinkers.

One trap here is that Thinkers may struggle to make a decision when "fairness" becomes too central to the final thought. They can become bogged down by trying to come up with a solution that feels balanced in a way that doesn't leave anyone out in the cold. Therefore, it is important for Thinkers to develop strategies for decision making that moves them along whenever the "fairness" question starts to interfere or shut down the process.

Finally, when it comes to focus and orientation, Thinkers prioritize:

- Things
- Truth
- Principles
- Solving problems

Thinkers can come across as task-oriented, uncaring or indifferent. So, it is important to develop interpersonal skills that focus on connecting with others, keeping the "people" part of a situation in view, and communicating your thoughts and decisions in a way that is firm but friendly.

Part 7: Being a Feeling Type

Think about a boss, professor or supervisor you enjoyed working with. What was it about them that made them effective?

If you said, "He was very attentive, he really took an interest in my future and wanted me to do my best, I could really trust him," you are likely a Feeling type ("Feeler").

This type is all about **what we base our decisions on.**

As a Feeler, you base your decisions on:

- Personal, values-oriented information
- What "feels right" and is likely to lead to a harmonious outcome
- Your impact on people

This means that your decision making process often keeps one eye on bottom lines but more of the focus is on how the decision will impact others and whether it will lead to contention and discord or connection and harmony. Feelers are very tuned in to their values and prefer making decisions that line up with these values independent of details, facts. In other words, "what feels right" will often outweigh "what makes sense."

At work and play, the Feeler:

- Is naturally friendly
- Acts personally
- Treats others uniquely and needs occasional praise
- Dislikes firing or reprimanding others
- Responds to people's values as much as to their thoughts

The Feeler has a natural ability to connect with others and discover what is distinct and unique about each individual. Feelers thrive best in friendships and work environments where verbal affirmations and feedback occur with some frequency.

One trap Feelers fall into is becoming personally connected to others in a way that makes it difficult to set boundaries or, in a work environment, reprimand or redirect employees. So, it is important for Feelers to strike a balance between "keeping the peace" and doing what is called for in a given situation—even if it means communicating a hard truth or leads to temporary disharmony.

Finally, when it comes to focus and orientation, Feelers prioritize:

- People
- Tact
- Harmony
- Supporting others

Feelers can come across as emotionally touchy or disconnected from logic. In reply to why they are doing or choosing something, it is not uncommon for a Feeler to say, "It just feels right." While this is a valid response, it can leave others feeling disconnected from your reasons. So, it is important for Feelers to develop the ability to clarify the underlying values or ideas that lead to them to the "feels right" conclusion. For example, a Feeler could say, "I really value our friendship, so it feels right that we spend more time together."

If you are a T interacting with a F:

- Don't immediately dismiss a Feeler for trusting his/her heart when making a decision
- Remember to offer praise and affirmation whenever possible

If you are a F interacting with a T:

- Don't immediately dismiss a Thinker for trusting his/her head when making a decision
- Resist the urge to label a Thinker as cold or disinterested simply because s/he focuses on logic or acts impersonally

Part 8: Being a Judging Type

How has parenting changed in the past 20 years?

If you said, "Well, you can list the changes in a spreadsheet and then rank them by what you believe is the most significant to understand exactly how parenting has changed," you are likely a Judging type.

This next type is all about **what our preferred lifestyle is.**

As a Judging type, your preferred lifestyle is:

- Organized
- Planned
- Oriented toward goals and results
- "The joy of closure"

This means that you thrive best when you have a plan, can spend time working through a project or event so as to gain a clear sense of all that will be involved before getting started, and really like reaching the end of something. Judging types are notorious for having checklists, spreadsheets, to do lists and working through them systematically.

You may find that you are more organized in one area of life more so than another or you may bring a sense of order and organization to every aspect of your life. Either way, when it comes to lifestyle, Judging types are keen to set up systems, put things in their "proper" place, and are elated by every task completed during the day.

At work and play, the Judging type is:

- Self-regimented
- Purposeful
- Exacting
- Focuses on completing the task
- Makes decisions quickly
- Uses lists
- Wants only essentials to begin projects

The Judging type is the person in the home or meeting that keeps things moving forward. Able to develop a plan with step-by-step action items, Judging types are often relied upon to keep projects and plans from become bogged down by indecision or running off track in a disorderly way.

One trap here is that Judging types can take on too much responsibility for planning. Other family members or co-workers will become overly reliant upon Judging types to first of all develop a plan and then oversee its implementation. This often results in Judging types resenting others for their lack luster ways and taking on too much. So, it is important for Judging types to learn to let go, in a way, and make room for others to take on some of the responsibility for either getting a project done, planning a vacation, or taking care of the home.

This usually requires Judging types avoid a second trap—thinking their way is the "right way." Since Judging types are so purposeful, exact, and self-regimented, they can often feel that the approach they have devised is sure proof and the best of all possible choices. So, in order to create room for others to play, Judging types will have to let go of this sense of "rightness."

Finally, when it comes to pace and closure, Judging types:

- Hate loose ends
- Like closure
- Want to be clear about who is in control
- Want to state their commitments
- Want a clear schedule

Judging types can come across as regimented or unspontaneous. It is often nice when Judging types and Perceiving get together since it can lead to a nice balance between spontaneity and organization. Still, Judging types often need to learn how to let down their hair and just go with the flow. A change in plans is not the end of the world, even if it can feel that way!

Part 9: Being a Perceiving Type

How has parenting changed in the past 20 years?

If you said, "There are probably a lot of ways that it has changed, let's talk about that for a bit. And then halfway through the discussion you say, 'Let's come back to this – how about we go grab a beer?'" you are likely a Perceiving type.

This next type is all about **what our preferred lifestyle is.**

As a Perceiving type, your preferred lifestyle is:

- Flexible
- Spontaneous
- Oriented toward gathering information
- "The joy of processing"

This means that you thrive best when you are able to spend time collecting information, developing and exploring ideas. You enjoy the process of a project, noticing all of the moving parts, but are less tied to the closure that the Judging type craves. So, loose or open ends are easy to stomach and, in fact, often enjoyed. Perceiving types are known for their flexibility and spontaneity and are often looked to for those "moments of distraction" we all need when simply keeping our heads down and getting things done becomes too much.

At work and play, the Perceiving type is:

- Curious, tolerant, adaptable
- Wants to know all about a project before beginning
- Postpones decisions
- Works most efficiently under last-minute pressure

Perceiving types easily adapt to change. They are tolerant of work and play environments that do not have clear schedules or routines. In fact, Perceiving types will often attempt to shake things up if things do seem to be settling into a pattern. Perceiving types are very curious and you will often find them exploring many topics or activities at one time.

One trap here is that Perceiving types will hesitate to make decisions because they want to remain open to respond to whatever happens. This can cause high levels of stress for you and others when deadlines are approaching or decisions are needed in order to move forward. Some of your best work will be done as a result of an approaching deadline or last-minute pressure. However, Perceiving types must learn to bring their same creativity and focus that arises at the eleventh hour to the other hours of the day as well when needed.

Finally, when it comes to pace and closure, Perceiving types:

- Resist closure
- Like to keep their options open
- Comment on the process
- Dislike schedules
- Often have last minute changes

Perceiving types can come across as procrastinators and unreliable. Perceiving types really like to discuss the project, plan for the project, get a sense of the project (or trip, or experience), but often have a hard time actually *starting* the project. As a result, they often leave things until the last minute. So, it is important for Perceiving types to develop a few strategies for reigning in these tendencies, especially when working to meet deadlines. One strategy is to set a hard time limit for how long a brainstorming or research time will last. Once that time is past, a decision has to be made!

While your preference in most areas of life might be to remain flexible and spontaneous (and this can be a real strength since it helps you remain open to new experiences and adapt to the world rather than organizing it), you are in fact, internally, usually very decisive, so you must learn to communicate this to the external world to balance perceptions of you as being flighty, unreliable, or indecisive.

If you are a J interacting with a P:

- As you are creating a plan, schedule, project, actually schedule in time for the P to gather information and then set a date for when the "exploration" phase is over and the "action" phase will begin
- Learn to trust that the P will come through—even if at the very last minute
- Give P's a "fake deadline." If you know, because you are a J and have timed everything perfectly, that you need to leave for the play by 7p at the latest, tell your P that you need to leave by 6:30p
- Embrace the P's spontaneity for your benefit—letting go of your plan/schedule can sometimes lead to a lot of fun, creativity or adventure

If you are a P interacting with a J:

- Learn to trust that the J's planning or scheduling is not an attempt to limit you or tie you down—keep breathing—it is just a plan
- Communicate clearly the decisions you are making internally, even if they don't lead to actionable behavior so that others know you are still engaged and not just wasting time
- Embrace the J's self-regimentation for your benefit—letting go of your tendency to resist closure can lead to accomplishment, clarity, and make room for new adventures

Part 10: Conclusion

I do want to make one observation in closing. We may be a very strong Judging type while being a middle of the road Intuitive. In some situations, we may tap into our Extrovert skills while remaining, at heart, in Introvert. In other words, it is important to keep in mind that we all share aspects of each personality type and, while presented in a binary kind of way, personality is best thought of in terms of a spectrum.

I hope you have enjoyed this overview and my attempt to highlight key characteristics and tendencies of behavior and perception that are commonly shared among those with a particular personality type. Remember to keep in mind the personality type "traps" and skills for getting along with each other!

About the Author

Rachel Grant is the owner and founder of Rachel Grant Coaching and is a Trauma Recovery and Relationship Coach. She is also the author of <u>Beyond Surviving: The Final Stage in Recovery from Sexual Abuse.</u>

She developed her Trauma Recovery and Relationship coaching programs based on her educational training and lessons learned from her own journey. She has been successfully working with clients since 2007.

Rachel holds an M.A. in Counseling Psychology. With this training in human behavior and cognitive development, she provides a compassionate and challenging approach for her clients while using coaching as opposed to therapeutic models. She is a member of the International Coach Federation and San Francisco Coaches.

If you would like to learn more about how coaching can support you in:

- Understanding who you are
- Transforming your thought life and relationships
- Overcoming the effects of past abuse
- Gaining new perspective that brings about action and change
- Clarifying and setting goals and seeing measurable results

Visit **www.rachelgrantcoaching.com** to schedule a FREE 60 minute Discovery Session.

Contact me at **coach@rachelgrantcoaching.com** or 415-513-0700

Printed in Great Britain
by Amazon.co.uk, Ltd.,
Marston Gate.